All About

SEALS, SEA LIONS and WALRUSES

A SEA WORLD BOOK ™

© 1994 Sea World, Inc. All Rights Reserved

Sea World, the Whale Logo, and the Sea World Characters are trademarks of Sea World, Inc.
No part of this book may be reproduced or copied in any form or by any means –
graphics, electronic, or mechanical, including photo copying, taping, or information storage and
retrieval systems – without written permission of the publisher.

Published by

THIRD STORY BOOKS
955 Connecticut Avenue, Suite 1302
Bridgeport, Connecticut 06607

ISBN 1-884506-13-5

Distributed to the trade by
Andrews & McMeel
4900 Main Street
Kansas City, Missouri 64112

Library of Congress Catalog Card Number: 94-6074

All photographs used courtesy of Sea World,
except the following:
Mark Conlin: pages 8, 10, 11 bottom, 14, 15 right, 16, 17 bottom, 20, 21.
Howard Hall Productions: pages 6, 24.
Daniel K. Odell, PhD: pages 11 top, 17 top.

Printed in Singapore

All About

SEALS, SEA LIONS and WALRUSES

Written by Jane Resnick

FEATURING *SeaWorld*® PHOTOGRAPHY

THIRD™
STORY
BOOKS

The tooth's the thing. Only one pinniped has tusks and that's the walrus. Tusks are actually huge canine teeth. Both male and female walruses have them.

Like humans, pinnipeds are mammals. They breathe air and are warm-blooded. They give birth to live babies and nurse their young. But pinnipeds live in and around the ocean and get their food at sea. That makes them *marine* mammals, like whales and sea otters.

■ Seals, sea lions and walruses are the marine animals with flippers. They're the three families of the scientific group *Pinnipedia*, which is Latin for "fin-footed." Over 30 species of pinnipeds live in different habitats all over the world. Pinnipeds exist both on land and in water.

FIN-FOOTED AND FABULOUS

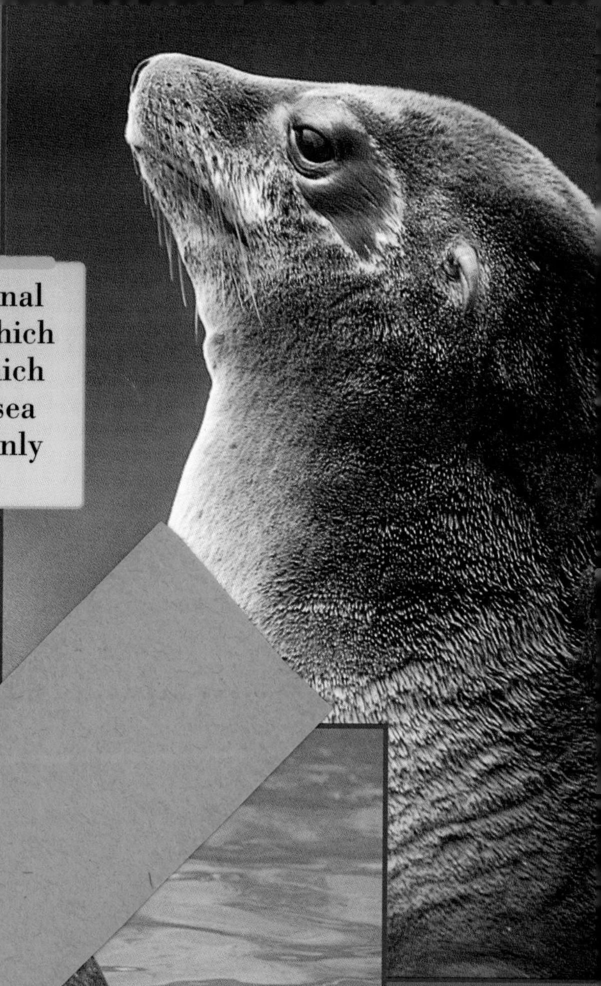

"Eared seals" have a small external ear. Among them are fur seals, which have a thick undercoat of fur which works to keep them warm, and sea lions (shown here), which have only a thin coat of underfur.

"Tr_____ ____ ____rbor seals, have tiny ear opening_ ____ ____ ____ flaps. Harbor seals have little or no ne____ ____ ____ore rounded heads than eared seals.

DOUBLE LIVES

■ At home in the water, yet unable to abandon land, pinnipeds live in two worlds. They're built for swimming and diving. They're dependent on the sea for food and spend most of their lives there. But they clamber onto rocky shores, sandy beaches and even ice floes to rest, molt, give birth, nurse their young and often to mate.

Pinnipeds have a unique circulatory system in their flippers, called a counter-current system. Flippering (sticking a flipper out of the water) may help them warm up.

These sea lions are flippering.

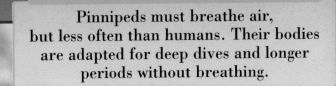

Pinnipeds must breathe air,
but less often than humans. Their bodies
are adapted for deep dives and longer
periods without breathing.

Streamlined is the
word for a pinniped.
Round and tapered at
both ends, its shape is
ideal for swooping
through water.

■ Pinnipeds have
a thick layer of fat,
called blubber,
under their skin.
Blubber contributes
to their sleek shape
and stores energy.
But most of all,
blubber acts as
insulation, holding
on to body heat in
cold water.

SEAWORTHY

A sea lion pup, flippers in view, takes in the Mexican sun.

■ Today's pinnipeds are descended from bearlike ancestors that existed over 20 million years ago. Most likely, they once had fore limbs and hind limbs that since have been modified for swimming into what are now called flippers. Seals, sea lions and walruses are still predators and they remain carnivores, which are meat-eaters. But their hunting ground is the sea and their prey are fish and squid.

How do you tell the difference between a seal and a sea lion?

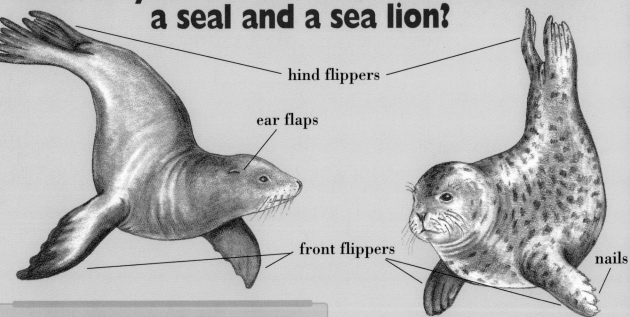

hind flippers

ear flaps

front flippers

nails

sea lion and fur seal

HEAD: has small, slim external ear flaps.

FRONT FLIPPERS: long and winglike; usually hairless. No noticeable nails.

HIND FLIPPERS: large and paddlelike; hairless; webbed digits. Nails midway along middle three digits. Can turn hind flippers forward for locomotion on land.

seal

HEAD: has tiny ear holes; no ear flaps.

FRONT FLIPPERS: short and blunt; with hair. Clawlike nails on digits.

HIND FLIPPERS: short and paddlelike; covered with hair; webbed digits. Nails on all digits. Can't turn hind flippers forward.

Graceful swimmers, pinnipeds are less mobile on land. Eared seals can turn their rear flippers forward and waddle on all fours. But true seals are crawlers. Their back flippers haven't much use on shore. So they scrunch up their bodies and move forward like giant, fat caterpillars.

HOMECOMING

■ Pinnipeds are most at home in the water, but if they do have a real home, it's the place where they breed. Year after year, they return to the same general area to give birth and mate. For certain species this journey is a migration of thousands of miles. Some come back to the exact beach where they were born.

A rookery is the place where colonies of pinnipeds – sometimes thousands – gather to mate and give birth. This is a California sea lion rookery in Mexico.

A northern (Alaskan) fur seal bull that has gathered a group of females for mating will defend them against the approach of any other male – fiercely.

When they arrive on shore, female pinnipeds give birth to one pup. The female becomes pregnant a year before the pup is born. The fertilized egg that rests in the mother's womb won't begin to grow for several months.

Young male northern elephant seals practice scare tactics. They roar. They stare sideways. They lunge. When they get older they may use these tactics before actually fighting.

11

WHAT'S UP WITH PINNIPED PUPS?

Walrus calves weigh about 130 to 140 pounds and are about three-and-a-half feet long when they are born. And that's *before* they fatten up.

The parents of pups don't stay together as families. Only the mothers care for the young. When the pups are weaned (no longer depend on their mothers' milk), they are called weaners and form groups of their own. Mothers and pups often rely on their smells to find each other. Cows also vocalize and babies bleat, so they can call to one another.

When pinniped pups are born, their eyes are open and their flippers are strong enough to be useful. Some, like the harbor seal, are able to swim within hours of their birth. Others may take several weeks. Because it is a mammal, a pup's first food is its mother's milk. Some pinnipeds, like the hooded seal, may nurse only three or four days. Others may stay with their mothers for over a year.

Pinnipeds are lucky pups. This sea lion's mother's milk is rich in fat. It helps the pup build up blubber and grow quickly.

One of the ways mothers and pups can find each other in crowded rookeries is by smell. Here, mother and pup get to know each other's smell.

13

Harbor seals get their name from where they live – harbors.

Harbor seals like to stick close to home. Unlike many pinnipeds, they typically prefer shallow or coastal waters and apparently don't take long migrations.

■ Among true or "earless" seals, harbor seals are one of the pretty pinnipeds. They have doglike faces with dark, gentle eyes. Their heads are round and their whiskers stick out like stiff spaghetti. Their coats shimmer in the water and blend in like boulders on the beach. But don't try to hug one. Harbor seals are very shy.

THE TRUE STORY

To see in the sea is not easy. It's dark. It's murky. But this harbor seal has mirrorlike membranes at the back of its eyes that reflect light which makes the sea around it seem brighter.

A harbor seal pup like this one is safe from predators at Sea World. Although mothers try hard to protect their pups in the wild, many don't survive once they're on their own.

LIONS AMONG SEALS

■ Sea lions are five of the 13 species of eared seals. The rest are called fur seals because they have dense fur coats. Sea lions swim very well. The California sea lion, for example, can swim at least 12 miles an hour in the wild, and can ride the surf.

Every summer a group of northern (Alaskan) fur seals migrates to the Pribilof Islands off the coast of Alaska. At one time almost a million-and-a-half seals swam to these rocky shores. Although the number is smaller now, it is still one of the largest gatherings of wild animals in any one place in the world.

Sea lions can walk on land because their hind flippers "turn around." They can take off, too, in a lopsided run.

A California sea lion rookery is a sociable place. Older animals breed and the younger ones play.

California sea lions are the speedy pinnipeds. Under zoological conditions, they have been reported swimming at 25 miles an hour.

ONE OF A KIND

Walruses don't chase after fish like other pinnipeds. In shallow waters, they search the ocean floor for food. Worms, clams and other shellfish are their prey. And walruses have a unique way of eating clams. After crushing their shells, they suck them right out and swallow them whole.

■ Among pinnipeds, the walrus is in a class by itself. Coated with some six inches of blubber, the walrus spends most of its life in frigid waters. Herds migrate together, hitchhiking rides on ice floes. Resting on rocky beaches, they pile up in bellowing masses.

Walrus calves are born without visible tusks, and for about two years their mothers take care of them.

As many as 700 whiskers bristle off a walrus's face. These are working whiskers. Like sensitive antennae, they help a walrus feel for food along the bottom of the sea.

Walruses sometimes use their tusks to anchor themselves as they haul out from the water onto ice.

■ The scientific name for walrus is Odobenus, Greek for "tooth-walker." Indeed, tusks are the walrus's most striking feature. They can be more than two feet long. Bulls show them off to display their superiority. Both sexes use them against their natural enemies, polar bears and killer whales.

■ They're big. They're loud. They're fierce. And boy, are they strange looking! Elephant seals are pinnipeds with presence. Like prehistoric monsters, they have thick, scarred skin and a truly weird nose that gives them their name. Males are huge. They can weigh 5,000 pounds and grow to 16 feet long. Females weigh less than 2,000 pounds and measure only about 10 feet long.

Elephant seals gather in a colony to mate, but it's not necessarily a friendly place because males tend to defend the area occupied by females. An area occupied by a large group of females might be shared by several males. Breeding males are often called "beachmasters."

Proboscis is the name for the male elephant seal's long, flexible, trunklike snout.

SUPER SEAL

To show who's boss, strong bulls throw back their heads and make an unearthly, pulsing sound. Weaker males will head for cover when they hear it. Braver fellows will fight, nose-to-nose, for the top spot.

Thanks to the mother's rich milk, pups can gain almost 12 pounds a day. A one-month-old elephant seal can weigh over 350 pounds!

Unlike the leopard seal, this crabeater seal doesn't eat Adélie penguins.
Do you think these penguins know that?

■ Brrr! Cold climates are home to many pinnipeds. Waters off Alaska are perfect for the Steller sea lion. The Antarctic is cozy enough for the crabeater and leopard seals. Leopard seals, like the cat they're named for, are stealthy hunters. They hide, sneak up and pounce on their prey. Their victims: penguins and other seals.

There are more than five million crabeater seals in antarctic waters. Their favorite food is tiny shrimplike animals called krill. And because this seal weighs about 500 pounds, and krill are only about two inches long, it takes a lot of krill to fill a crabeater seal.

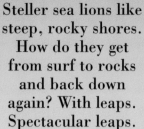

Steller sea lions like steep, rocky shores. How do they get from surf to rocks and back down again? With leaps. Spectacular leaps.

Although the leopard seal may appear to be harmless, it is one of the fiercest pinnipeds.

DIFFERENT AND THE SAME

The male hooded seal is unique. It can inflate its nose to form a black "hood," or it can also inflate the red inner lining of its nose to form a "balloon." The hood or the balloon may be used to attract females or to signal the seal's presence to other males.

■ The different species of pinnipeds are similar but not the same. While many pinnipeds gather in large groups, some, like Arctic bearded seals, are less likely to gather in groups. Although seals come to shore to breed, harp seals choose offshore ice. A plain brown coat is common to many pinnipeds, but the ribbon seal and the ringed seal get their names from patterns in their fur.

Male Australian sea lions are chocolate brown. Females (like this one) are gray to tan.

The male South American sea lion has a great mane like a lion.

A hooded seal without an inflated nose.

25

CURTAIN UP!

■ Walruses are extremely inquisitive and are considered fast swimmers. California sea lions are quick and playful. A trained sea lion can catch a Frisbee. At Sea World pinnipeds are carefully, gently trained through positive reinforcement. They learn a whole range of behaviors that they appear to enjoy performing and people enjoy watching and learning from.

At Sea World pinnipeds learn to do complicated behaviors in small steps. When they perform, their trainer usually gives them a sign that tells them what to do. One of the most complicated behaviors sea lions learn is to perform on stage alone – without a trainer guiding them.

Hi there! One of the behaviors that delight audiences is a wave from a walrus.

Pinnipeds demonstrate many different behaviors in shows that have plots, action, and humor, as well as an environmental message.

A sea lion helps a pirate read a treasure map.

LIFE AT SEA WORLD

■ More than a hundred pinnipeds live at each Sea World location and most all of them are born there. They spend their days in a natural rocky shore habitat with large swimming pools and deck space. They even have "sun rooms," dry areas where they can haul out and bask in the sunshine.

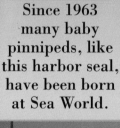

Since 1963 many baby pinnipeds, like this harbor seal, have been born at Sea World.

Pacific Point Preserve at Sea World of Florida.

Some wild pinnipeds are temporary guests at Sea World. When they are found on beaches, either sick or injured, they are brought to Sea World where, with shelter, care and rest, they get a chance to recover. When they are well and strong, they're brought back to the wild.

Pinnipeds, like this hooded seal, eat huge amounts of fish every day. Walruses even get their favorite – clams, already shelled!

29

FASCINATING FACTS

Blubber Boy - The giant southern bull elephant seal can weigh 8,500 pounds, more than four tons!

Miles of Insides - Sea lions have very long intestines. If a Steller sea lion's intestines were uncoiled, they could stretch to about 250 feet long – and that would be about 38 times the animal's body length.

Body Heat - Pinnipeds swimming in freezing sea water can have an inside body temperature of 99 degrees F.

Depth Charger - Dives of some 5,000 feet have been recorded by elephant seals, the deepest pinniped divers.

Breathless - When people dive, they breathe in first. Pinnipeds usually breathe out. Much of the oxygen they will need while underwater is stored in their blood and muscles, not their lungs. Elephant seals have been known to stay underwater for up to 80 minutes.

No Snoring - Some seals sleep under water. Breathing is automatic. When necessary, they unconsciously come up for air.

Furry Fellows - Eared pinnipeds have two types of hair. One type is the underfur that keeps them warm. The other type is called guard hair. The thick underfur on fur seals can contain up to 300,000 hairs per square inch.

GLOSSARY

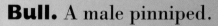

Bellow. To make a loud, deep sound.

Bull. A male pinniped.

Calf. A newborn walrus.

Canine teeth. The two pointed upper teeth on either side of the four front teeth.

Clamber. To climb awkwardly, as over rocks.

Colony. The group of pinnipeds that gathers in a rookery.

Cow. A female pinniped.

Flippers. Limbs modified for swimming. Seals have four webbed, paddlelike flippers.

Habitat. The place where an animal naturally lives.

Harbor. A protected body of water such as where fishermen dock their boats.

Harem. The group of females that lives in the territory of a male or males.

Haul out. The term used when pinnipeds come out of the water onto land or ice.

Ice floes. Flat, floating pieces of ice.

Intestine. A tube coming from the stomach that food passes through.

Membrane. A thin, tough layer of tissue.

Migrate. To move from one region to another for feeding or breeding.

Molt. To shed an old coat of fur and grow a new one.

Nurse. In female mammals, to give milk to young.

Predator. An animal that hunts and eats other animals.

Pup. The young of all pinnipeds. However, walrus babies are usually called calves.

Snout. A long nose that juts forward.

Squid. A shellfish with a thin body and eight short arms.

A Sea World
B O O K ™

> "For in the end we will conserve only what we love.
> We will love only what we understand.
> And we will understand only what we are taught."
> *Baba Dioum – noted Central African Naturalist*

About the Author

Jane Resnick is a writer with a special interest in oceans and rivers and the creatures who live there. Her experiences canoeing with her family on wilderness rivers and exploring sea coasts all over America have been the subjects of many articles. She has written many wonderful books for children including *Fish*, a book about the undersea world, *All About Sharks*, a look at one of the most interesting animals on earth, and *All About Training Shamu*, a fascinating exploration of how the world's most famous killer whale learned to work with humans. Jane lives in Connecticut on a lake (of course) with her family and two Labrador Retrievers.

THIRD STORY BOOKS